Teen Survival Guides

Learning to Be Self-Aware

JENNIFER SANDERSON

CHERITON
CHILDREN'S BOOKS

Published in 2026 by **Cheriton Children's Books**
1 Bank Drive West, Shrewsbury, Shropshire, SY3 9DJ, UK

First Edition

Author: Jennifer Sanderson
Designer: Paul Myerscough
Editor: Kelly Short
Proofreader: Amy Strauss

Picture credits: Cover: Shutterstock/Mentatdgt. Inside: p4: Shutterstock/SeventyFour, p5: Shutterstock/Ground Picture, p6: Shutterstock/Prostock Studio, p7: Shutterstock/MPH Photos, p8: Shutterstock/Vk St, p9: Shutterstock/Alberto Menendez Cervero, p11: Shutterstock/Lomb, p13: Shutterstock/Carlos Barquero, p14: Shutterstock/Monkey Business Images, p15: Shutterstock/PeopleImages.com/Yuri A, p16: Shutterstock/Lordn, p17: Shutterstock/Monkey Business Images, p19: Shutterstock/Pheelings Media, p20: Shutterstock/Prostock Studio, p23: Shutterstock/LightField Studios, p24: Shutterstock/Basicdog, p25: Shutterstock/Monkey Business Images, p27: Shutterstock/Suzanne Tucker, p28: Shutterstock/MalikNalik, p29: Shutterstock/Inside Creative House, p30: Shutterstock/Monkey Business Images, p31: Shutterstock/Miljan Zivkovic, p33: Shutterstock/Fizkes, p34: Shutterstock/Ground Picture, p36: Shutterstock/Denisart, p37: Shutterstock/PeopleImages.com/Yuri A, p38: Shutterstock/Julia Shepeleva, p39: Shutterstock/Kaspars Grinvalds, p40: Shutterstock/EF Stock, p41: Shutterstock/VH Studio, p43: Shutterstock/VH Studio, p45: Shutterstock/TimeImage Production, p46: Shutterstock/Rawpixel.com, p47: Shutterstock/Gonzagon, p48: Shutterstock/Gumpanat, p49: Shutterstock/Maples Images, p51: Shutterstock/Lopolo, p52: Shutterstock/Suzanne Tucker, p53: Shutterstock/TimeImage Production, p54: Shutterstock/Rawpixel.com, p57: Shutterstock/Perfect Wave, p58: Shutterstock/Pics Five, p59: Shutterstock/Namart Pieamsuwan.

Printed in China

Please visit our website,
www.cheritonchildrensbooks.com
to see more of our high-quality books.

Contents

INTRODUCTION

Being Self-Aware

Since you've become a teenager, your life has probably changed a lot. To begin with, your body may be changing, and that can be hard to get used to. These physical changes may make you very self-conscious. You may feel like everyone is looking at you and talking about your new, more-adult body. Your hormones may also be making you a lot more emotional, and suddenly things that never bothered you before may be really upsetting. It may feel like the world is a big, scary place. The truth is, the world is a big place—but that means it is full of great possibilities. And within this big world, you are going to find your place by learning new skills that will help you be more self-aware.

Taking on a challenge can feel tough. But when you achieve what you set out to do, you'll feel really proud of yourself.

Self-awareness skills will help you find your place in the world.

STUDIES IN TEEN SURVIVAL

Your teenage years are a bit like a roller coaster ride, with many ups and downs. There are also a lot of changes happening. You're probably trying to figure out who you are. You're likely discovering what you believe in, and what your values are. You might feel more impulsive than you did in the past. And your hormones can make you feel happy, sad, and even both at the same time. Being self-aware can help you navigate this bumpy ride.

Skills for Life

Being aware of something means you know it well. Self-awareness is about getting to know yourself—really well. It includes knowing what your values are and what is important to you. Self-awareness means getting to know your feelings, strengths, and weaknesses. It means discovering the effect that you have on other people in the world around you. Young people who are self-aware embrace the challenges that life throws at them with a positive mindset. There are ten self-awareness skills that are important to master while you're a teenager. If you can get a handle on them, it will make being an adult much easier. So, let's get to the skills:

- **Self-reflection**
- **Embracing challenges**
- **Developing a growth mindset**
- **Building resilience**
- **Building confidence**
- **Self-assessment**
- **Accepting feedback**
- **Envisioning your future self**
- **Problem-solving**
- **Impact awareness**

We'll explain what these terms mean as we work through the book and explore them in workshops. By the time you've finished the book, you'll understand what they mean. And you'll have learned some important skills that you can use for the rest of your life.

CHAPTER 1

Know Yourself

You may have heard adults talking about teenagers and saying that the teens are "really emotional," but what exactly does that mean? Emotions are things you feel, and they cause you to react in a certain way. For example, when something good happens, you feel pleased, excited, or happy. These are positive emotions—you feel great inside. If something upsets you or makes you feel overwhelmed, these are negative feelings. Positive or negative, there are no right or wrong emotions. Every emotion that you feel is valid. And every emotion someone else feels is valid too.

You Have an Attitude!

When you use an emotion to underpin how you think or feel about something it's called an attitude. For example, if you enjoy school and have mostly happy experiences there, your teachers may say you have a positive attitude to school. On the flip side, if for example, you don't enjoy exercise, your gym teacher may tell you that you have an apathetic attitude toward his class. This means you do not care about it a lot. Everyone has different attitudes, and like emotions, all are valid.

When you're self-aware, you better understand what triggers you and you understand your emotions better.

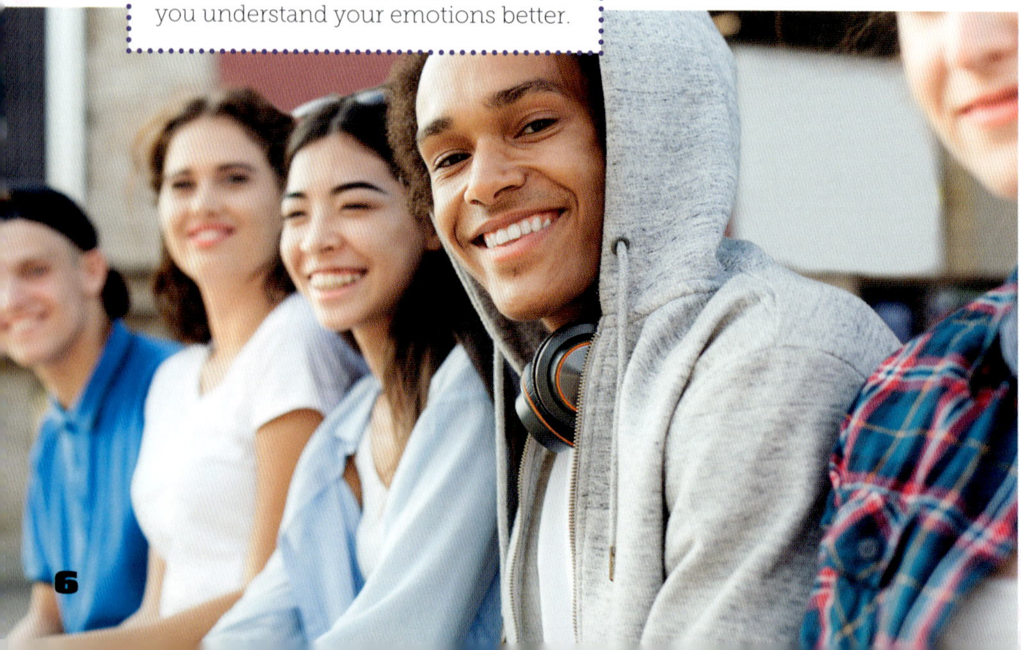

Be Positive

It's impossible to be positive ALL the time, but trying to have a positive attitude has many benefits. To begin with, you'll be more productive. You'll do more and fit in more. You'll also be less stressed, and being less stressed means overall your wellbeing will improve. You'll be less likely to struggle, and be less likely to experience depression. You'll also feel more confident (there'll be more about this in the next chapter).

Teen Need to Know

Academic success can be linked to your attitude. If you have a positive attitude to learning, you will be more relaxed at school. And, if you're more relaxed, you'll be able to absorb and remember the information you learn. Being relaxed helps you focus too. If you have a positive attitude, you'll see your classes as an opportunity to learn rather than a chore.

A Problem-Busting Tool

Being Grateful

One of the ways to develop a more positive outlook is to develop an attitude of gratitude. This means being grateful for the things you have, rather than the things you don't. Even when you feel that everything is going wrong, there is always something to feel grateful for. You may just have to think a little harder to realize it.

Expressing your gratitude is good for relationships. Take some time to tell the people you care about that you are grateful for them.

Let's Talk about Self-Reflection

We live in a really busy world. It's fast-paced and demanding, and there are probably days where it feels like everyone wants a piece of you. The worst part is that you may not actually know what you want. You may just try to please everyone else and tick all the boxes to keep them happy. However, that may not help you to be happy, and it can make everything feel very overwhelming. It can also leave you feeling really frustrated. When that happens, you need to take time out, reflect, and think about how you feel about things.

It's natural to feel overwhelmed every now and again. If you take time out to self-reflect, you'll feel a lot better for it.

Defining Self-Awareness Skills: Self-Reflection

Reflecting means you take a step back and think about things. So self-reflection means you think about yourself. When you reflect on yourself, you become more aware of your behavior, thoughts, attitudes, and emotions. Self-reflection is a way to get to know yourself better so that you make good, thought-through decisions.

THE SELF-AWARENESS WORKSHOP

Not Taking Time for Self-Reflection

There are many scenarios in which not taking time to self-reflect can cause bumps in the road. For example, imagine you are not good with crowds and busy places. Then imagine your best friend invites you to celebrate their birthday at a theme park. All your friendship group will be there. You hate fast rides and big crowds, but you feel like you should just go along with it. And you want to be part of the group. So you say, "Yes, great, I'll come." At the theme park, everyone else looks like they are having fun as they line up for the roller coaster. But you feel really anxious. Your palms are sweating and you feel sick. You get on the ride, and it seems to last forever. All the time you hate it. When you finally get off the ride, you just want to go home. And you wish you hadn't gone.

In this situation, you didn't take time to think about how you would feel once the situation became a reality. With some self-reflection, things could have been a lot easier. Let's take a look overleaf.

THE SELF-AWARENESS WORKSHOP

Same situation, but with self-reflection.

Taking Time to Reflect

When your best friend invites you to celebrate their birthday at a theme park, you stop and think before you say, "Yes!" straight up. You know you hate fast rides and big crowds, but you want to be part of the group—all your friends are going. So, you tell your best friend that you'd love to come but the rides really scare you. You suggest that you watch everyone else go on them, though. Your friend says, "I understand, and it's a good plan." You feel relieved. You then enjoy the day without being stressed.

What Works Better Here?:

- You think about the day and realize that the idea of the rides stresses you out.
- You explain your feelings to your friend. They understand and see your viewpoint.
- You find a way to enjoy the day, and join in, without it causing anxiety.

Knowing Yourself—What Can It Do for You?

Sometimes, you realize that doing things to fit in with others can make you feel uncomfortable. If you take time to self-reflect and think about how you feel, you can take action ahead of time to reduce your anxiety. By being honest with yourself and others, you can figure out a plan to deal with the situation effectively, and have a great time as a result.

Taking time to self-reflect may feel strange at first but you'll be amazed at how much better it will make you feel after a while.

A PROBLEM-BUSTING TOOL

Self-Reflection Checklist

To know yourself better and really reflect on things, try to answer these questions:

- **Check your mind:** How do you feel? Do you feel clear-headed? Is there something that you're finding really challenging at school or at home?
- **Check your body:** Do you feel physically strong and able? Do you feel healthy? Do you feel exhausted? What's made you feel this way? How can you change it?
- **Check in with yourself:** Do you feel at peace? Are you connected to the world around you? Are you feeling agitated or irritated?
- **Check your social life**: Are you doing things that make you happy or that make you sad?
- **Check your relationships:** Are your friendships happy and healthy or is there something bothering you? What is your relationship like with your parents, and your siblings? Could it be better? How?

Try to do this exercise as often as you can manage.

STUDIES IN TEEN SURVIVAL

Studies have shown that self-reflection helps students learn. It helps you develop a growth mindset (you'll find out more about growth mindsets later). It also helps you learn from your mistakes.

WHY SELF-AWARENESS WORKS

Self-awareness starts with getting to know yourself. Let's take another look at why self-reflection is important.

1 Personal Growth Is Linked to Your Attitude

A positive attitude encourages learning and growth. When you try your best to have a good attitude, you'll be more open to learning. When you have a positive attitude to your schoolwork, your grades will improve.

2 Grateful People See the Good, Even in Difficult Situations

Instead of focusing on the bad, grateful people try to find a positive in every situation they experience.

3 Knowing Yourself Helps You Make Better Decisions

When we are aware of our experiences, we can use this awareness to make better decisions in the future.

4 Self-Reflection Keeps You Focused

When you spend time thinking about things, you get to know yourself and you stay focused on what's important to you.

Better Relationships

Relationships are better when you know yourself. When you know yourself, you are honest about how you feel about a situation or another person's actions. You know what you do or don't like. You understand what you will or won't accept. If something is not for you, you can say so. However, try to be considerate of others and try to explain yourself clearly and without being angry. If you feel upset about something, take a deep breath and start by saying, "I feel..."

CHAPTER 2

You and Your Family: A Survival Guide

Families can come in many different shapes and sizes. They're usually made up of parents/caregivers and siblings, but there are no hard-and-fast rules. Families can be made up of just one parent and no siblings or stepparents. They can include stepsiblings as well as half-siblings. Sometimes, extended families that are made up of grandparents—and possibly even aunts and uncles—also live together. Whatever the makeup of your family, each person in it is unique and has their own personality. All these different personalities under one roof can be great when everyone gets along. However, it's not so great when there are problems.

Family Problems

All relationships have their ups and downs. That's natural. Some days, your siblings will be your best friends. Other days, you wish they'd leave you alone. The problem is, that's probably not going to happen. If you're living under the same roof, it's impossible to avoid each other permanently. Sooner or later, you'll need to come together again and interact with one another.

Talking through problems with your family is a great way to develop your self-awareness skills.

A Self-Aware Family

How family members interact with one another depends a lot on how self-aware each family member is. When people are self-aware, they know their own strengths and weaknesses. Everyone is able to be the best version of themselves. This also means that each person is accepted for who they are. Self-aware families talk openly about difficult subjects. That's because everyone's opinion matters and all opinions are valid. People are allowed to feel emotions and express their emotions. So if being self-aware is the key to a harmonious family life, how do you and your family members become more self-aware?

Learning the Skills

To become more self-aware, you can start with some self-reflection. You could encourage your family members to do the Self-Reflection Problem-Busting exercise in chapter one, too. Added to this, you and your family can focus on learning some new self-awareness skills that bring benefits to any family. These super skills are embracing challenges, developing a growth mindset, and building resilience. We'll look at the skills in more detail in this chapter.

Although you may find your siblings a little irritating from time to time, doing things with them can be fun.

STUDIES IN TEEN SURVIVAL

Studies have shown that family relationships play a very important role in teenagers' development into adults. How teenagers interact, or don't interact, with family members determines their viewpoints. It shapes their values, relationships, and understanding of themselves. Simply put, their interactions shape their self-awareness.

Sometimes, a challenge such as your family relocating feels like the end of the world. But with a positive attitude you will find your feet quickly.

It's a Stressful Time

Being a teenager can be challenging. There's probably a lot going on at your school, in your friendship circle, and in your family at home too. As you grow older, you are probably becoming more aware of problems at home. This may be because your parents tell you more—they may feel you are old enough and mature enough to know some of their struggles. Or it may be because you are more in tune with your family members and so are more empathetic to what is happening to them.

Let's Talk about Embracing Challenges

Sometimes, there are challenges that affect the whole family. Perhaps your parents are getting divorced or maybe your family has to relocate. There could also be problems that affect just one person in the family. Perhaps a sibling is struggling at school. Sometimes, challenges last a little longer than a couple of days. When the going gets tough, you have two options. You can try and hide in your room or you can embrace the challenges.

Defining Self-Awareness Skills: Embracing Challenges

To embrace challenges means to accept and acknowledge any difficulties or setbacks, and use them as opportunities for growth. Instead of hiding away and feeling sorry for yourself, you think about the situation and try to find positives in it. When you embrace challenges, you see how you can use them to become a better, stronger version of yourself.

THE SELF-AWARENESS WORKSHOP

Avoiding the Challenge

Avoiding challenges can just make problems worse. More often than not, they grow bigger and get out of control. For example, imagine one of your parents is offered a job in a new location. It's a great opportunity—more money and better prospects. But it means you have to move and leave behind your school and friends. You are really not happy about that. So you tell your parents, "I'm not going! My life is here." You threaten to go and live with your best friend rather than having to move. This causes a lot of upset for your mom and dad. They feel really stressed, and worried about taking the job.

You feel upset because you don't want to go. But you haven't really thought through the situation and all its positives. There could be big benefits for both you and your parents. If you rise to the challenge, it could be great for you all...

THE SELF-AWARENESS WORKSHOP

Same situation, but rising to the challenge.

Embracing the Challenge

Your parents tell you that one of them has been offered a job in a new location. It's a great opportunity—more money and better prospects. But it means you will have to move and leave behind your school and friends. You feel worried about that. You talk to your best friend, and tell them, "I'm really scared. I don't want to lose you." They say, "It will be fine—we can still see each other on holidays and at weekends." You decide to make the best of it, and start finding out about your new town. Your mom and dad feel relieved. Together, you can start looking forward to the move.

What Works Better Here?:

- You try to see the positives in the situation.
- You talk about worries with your friend and they help you work through them.
- By being positive, you help your parents look forward and plan the future.

Embracing Challenges—What Can It Do for You?

When you embrace a challenge, you'll be able to find something positive in it. Sometimes, it's hard to do this on your own and you may need a bit of help from someone to see the good that a challenge can bring.

Keeping fit and healthy is a good way to physically deal with stress and challenges.

A PROBLEM-BUSTING TOOL

Dealing with a Challenging Time

When you are facing a challenge, take a deep breath and follow these steps:

- **Deal with your problems:** They won't go away on their own—identify the problem and form a plan to work on it.
- **Find balance:** Take time away from the challenge to do something you enjoy, even if it's a short break to walk your dog or listen to music.
- **Plan your day:** Make a list of what you need to do and tick off things as you get them done—it will make you feel more in control.
- **Ask for help:** When things get too challenging, ask for help from a trusted adult.
- **Eat healthy food:** Your diet affects your mood and your physical wellbeing.
- **Sleep well:** If you don't get enough sleep, you're more likely to feel stressed over the little things.
- **Exercise:** Exercising regularly is a good stressbuster because your brain floods your body with happy hormones.
- **Breathe:** Spend a few minutes throughout your day breathing deeply. Count from one to five as you inhale and from five to ten as you breathe out.

Keep a Flexible Mindset

You have seen how when you embrace your challenges, you try to be positive. And, by being positive, you'll hopefully learn from the challenge. Learning from a challenge is linked to the concept of neuroplasticity. Plasticity means something can be molded or altered, so what does neuroplasticity mean? Let's explore this intriguing term.

Let's Talk about Developing a Growth Mindset

Neuroplasticity is the brain's ability to be flexible and change as needed. When you learn new things or face challenges, the cells in the brain form new connections. The connections grow stronger with more practice and use. So if you overcome a challenge or practice a new skill again and again, your brain knows exactly what to do. This means that you get better at it and more used to it. A growth mindset uses this concept of neuroplasticity to learn from trying new things, and to grow and change.

The connections in your brain grow stronger each time you repeat something. This means each time you try something difficult, it will become easier.

Defining Self-Awareness Skills: Developing a Growth Mindset

A growth mindset views challenges as opportunities to grow and learn. If you have a growth mindset, you'll be more open to learning and improving your life. The thing is, growth mindsets are not only about being successful. If you have built a growth mindset and things don't work out as planned, you won't view this as a failure or a step backward. Instead, you'll see it as a chance to learn and improve. A growth mindset motivates you, making you more likely to get back up and try again.

The Value of Building a Growth Mindset

It can be hard to try new things, especially when you're worried about failing. Often, people like to play things safe for this very reason. When you are reluctant to try new things and to learn from challenges, it's called having a fixed mindset. Someone with a fixed mindset believes if they can't do something right first time around, they are not good at something and so there is no point in trying again. For example, they may try to windsurf for the first time, but fall into the water on the first attempt. They quickly give up, believing that they will never be able to windsurf. But a person with a growth mindset would realize it will take time and a lot of practice to learn this new skill. They may keep falling into the water, but they don't give up. They keep practicing and keep positive, realizing they are slowly improving. They get better and better, and eventually, they learn to windsurf.

STUDIES IN TEEN SURVIVAL

Research shows that teenagers with a growth mindset are more likely to choose activities that challenge them to learn new things. When you have a growth mindset, you want to learn and you want to try, even if it means not getting something right the first time around. This attitude helps you at school and in all aspects of your life.

Embracing Challenge

With a growth mindset, you realize that you are going to learn. With a growth mindset, you embrace your challenges as they arise. You keep working on skills, even if they seem difficult. You keep your end goal in mind, and remind yourself why you are putting in the effort to achieve it. With a strong growth mindset, almost anythng can be achieved.

The Benefits of Growth

There's more to a growth mindset than, for example, making the swim team and getting good grades. A growth mindset can be applied to everything in life. You can use a growth mindset to strengthen and improve relationships. For example, if you have a growth mindset and you do something to hurt a friend, you own up to your error. You apologize, and learn from your mistake so that you don't do it again. A growth mindset can also help you overcome a fear or phobia. If you are afraid of heights, for example, a growth mindset will help you try climbing, even though it may involve going high up. If you successfully conquer the height, your brain will learn that it's not so scary. You'll then be more willing to try it again. By having a growth mindset, you will be calm and confident. This is because you know that even if you cannot do something right now, you'll get there. If you have a growth mindset, solving problems is much easier too because you are not so frightened of failing.

A PROBLEM-BUSTING TOOL

Using Affirmations

One way to develop a strong growth mindset is to use positive affirmations. An affirmation is something you tell yourself, but it doesn't mean talking to yourself! Instead, you use your inner voice to overcome a fixed mindset. You change the negative voice in your head into a positive one. Positive self-talk builds confidence too, because you are focusing on what you do well rather than your failures. If you're new to affirmations, start with these:

- **I can do difficult things:** Life isn't always easy but you can tackle difficult things. If you don't succeed the first time, you can try again.
- **I can succeed with constant effort:** Keep working hard and you will reap the rewards.
- **I am not giving up:** It might be tempting to give up but if you persevere, you will succeed.
- **I am proud of my achievements:** Know what you've accomplished and be proud of your success. This will give you confidence to try new things.
- **If I practice, I will improve:** You don't need to be perfect, you just need to improve each time you practice something.
- **Mistakes help me grow:** Learn from your mistakes and move on.
- **I am strong and powerful:** When you feel strong, you will feel confident.

When something feels difficult, remind yourself that with practice, you'll get there.

Teen Need to Know

Saying affirmations may seem a little weird at first. However, studies have shown that when you do it regularly, you are actually training your brain. The training strengthens the connectivity between the different regions of the brain that deal with stressful situations, problem-solving skills, and creativity. It's a lot like building muscle in a gym—the more it's done, the stronger the connections become.

Let's Talk about Building Resilience

What do you do when a challenge comes your way and you've tried your best but you can't see a way through it? It seems like it's beyond your control and you'll never succeed. Well, in cases like these, you dig deep, tap into your newly found growth mindset, and build resilience.

Defining Self-Awareness Skills: Building Resilience

Resilience is the ability to bounce back during a challenging time. It's about more than just coping and simply hoping for the best. Resilience is a skill that will help you find ways to overcome your challenges and achieve your goals. When you are resilient, you take a growth mindset one step farther. You pick yourself up after a setback and you try again.

Resilient teens don't give up. They pick themselves up and try again.

Talking to your parents is a good way to build resilience. Your parents want you to succeed and will help you overcome a challenge.

Accept What You Cannot Change

Part of being resilient is knowing that you cannot always change things. It's about realizing that sometimes, you have to find a way of accepting things as they are. For example, if your parents are getting divorced, there is very little you can do about it. Acting out won't change their minds, and it may just create more tension. If you can try to understand your parents' situation, it'll make things a lot easier for you. As difficult as it is, try to embrace the challenge and see some positive in it.

Top Tips to Build Resilience

Sometimes, you may feel more resilient than at other times. How resilient you feel may depend on the situation. Some challenges are more difficult to bounce back from—for example, if there's a death in your family or you suddenly have to move home. To build resilience, it helps to have a good support network. Your parents and siblings are a good place to start when it comes to building a network. When things aren't great, they will have your back. Try to do one thing a day that gives you a sense of purpose and makes you feel good. If you feel confident, you'll be more likely to pick yourself up after a setback. If you do have a setback—and they are inevitable—try to think about instances in the past where you dealt with setbacks and succeeded. Then draw on those experiences. The key to being resilient is to stay hopeful. You can't change the past but you can hope for a better and brighter future.

WHY SELF-AWARENESS WORKS

Learning to be self-aware can seem complicated, but increased self-awareness has benefits for your whole family. This chapter has looked at three skills to help develop self-awareness: embracing challenges, developing a growth mindset, and building resilience.

1 Embracing Challenges Benefits Your Whole Family

When your family faces a challenge, you can work together to find the positives in a difficult situation.

2 A Growth Mindset Helps You Learn

Instead of feeling defeated and like you can't do something, a growth mindset gives you the confidence to try new things without fear of failure.

3 Affirmations Train Your Brain

By repeating positive self-talk, your brain's many connections will be strengthened. Your fixed mindset will slowly be replaced by a growth mindset.

4 Resilience Helps You Bounce Back

When you are resilient, you don't simply give up when you experience a setback. Instead, you do your best and try again.

In It for the Long Run

Although you may spend less time with your family now that you're a teenager, if you use these skills at home, your family life will improve. You may not appreciate that now, but you will as you grow older. You'll also develop these important skills and be able to apply them to other situations later in life.

CHAPTER 3

School, College, and Work

School is a busy time. You're expected to put effort into your schoolwork. You may participate in several sports and cultural activities after school. And you also want to spend more time with friends. You may also be thinking about what you want to do when you finish school and trying to form a plan of action. This can feel a little overwhelming sometimes. When it does, stop! Pause to think about who you are as a person and where you'd like to be. You don't need definite answers yet, just a rough idea to guide you. This is self-awareness at its best. By becoming more self-aware, your days will be less challenging.

The older you get, the busier your time at school or college will become. Working on your self-awareness skills will help you manage when you feel overwhelmed.

Keeping a journal is a great way to become more self-aware. It's also good for dealing with the stress that comes with a busy school life. By keeping a journal, you will be able to pick up on patterns of behavior.

Preparing for the Future

When you're self-aware, you know yourself better. You're more positive, and you also know your strengths and weaknesses. This can help you figure out strategies to succeed in your work and social life. But, there's no magic formula to suddenly becoming more self-aware. Developing self-awareness skills takes time and persistence. Try to start developing these now while at school so you can take them with you to college, and later to your work life.

Skills for Life

There are some important social-awareness skills that help you in your school, college, and work life. They are building confidence, self-assessment, accepting feedback, and envisioning your future self. If you can master these skills, you will be well prepared to face the day-to-day demands of school and college before you later head off into the workplace.

STUDIES IN TEEN SURVIVAL

Research shows that developing students' social and emotional mindsets may increase wellbeing and happiness. When you are happy at school, you do better academically. Studies also show that when you are self-aware, you behave better around others. You have fewer biases, and you are kinder and more helpful toward people. These are also important skills to take into the workplace.

Standing Tall

As a teenager, you'll have good days and bad days. This is normal. Everyone has ups and downs. On the good days, you feel like you're on top of the world. But sometimes, you have bad days. You may feel as though you can't do anything right. On those days, you may feel like hiding away. Often, these feelings of wanting to hide from the world relate to your confidence.

Let's Talk about Building Confidence

Confidence is about believing in yourself, your abilities, and ideas. It's about knowing something you suggest is a good idea, and being able to talk politely about your idea to others. When you are confident, you feel like you can take on challenges. You feel good about yourself, and you like and accept who you are. You don't feel the need to change to fit in with others.

Being confident makes you feel good about yourself.

Defining Self-Awareness Skills: Building Confidence

Building confidence means doing things that make you feel good about yourself and that you enjoy. It takes time and practice to build confidence, so start by doing one confidence-builder a day. Confidence builders include being kind to yourself. They also include spending time with people who love you. And in the list too is learning to assert yourself. This means saying what you really feel in a polite and kind way. Some days you may try to do all this and still feel lacking in confidence. Here's a tip: act confident! The saying "fake it until you make it" really works.

THE SELF-AWARENESS WORKSHOP

Lacking Confidence

Lacking confidence can have a big impact on your life. It can keep you from trying things that you might love or be great at. Imagine a scenario in which you want to get into a sports team—basketball, for example. The coach has seen you play and tells you that you are good. They think you can make it on to the team—there is a place. They say, "Why don't you try out?" But you feel worried about it. You really like basketball, but don't think you are good enough to play for the team. The coach explains that all you need are a few more training sessions to learn the game better and build up confidence. They can help you with training if you give it a go. You say, "I'll think about it. I'll come back to you tomorrow." But you never do. Then the space on the team is taken, and you feel you have lost out.

By not having the confidence to try, you missed an opportunity and felt disappointed. But what if you had tried for the team and taken a chance? Let's explore that overleaf.

THE SELF-AWARENESS WORKSHOP

Same situation, but with more confidence.

Gaining Confidence

You really want to get into the basketball team. The coach has seen you play, and tells you that you are good. They think you can make it on to the team—there is a place. They say, "Why don't you try out?" But you feel worried about it. The coach explains that you play well, and all you need are a few more training sessions to build up confidence. So you say, "OK. Sure." Then you train with them over the next few weeks. And when you try out for the team, you nail it. You feel great—and it is a boost for your confidence.

What Works Better Here?:

- You decide to give the training a go.
- The training boosts your confidence, so much so that you try out for the team.
- You win a place on the team. That makes you feel great and even more confident.

Building Confidence—What Can It Do for You?

You don't always feel confident about everything. But if you work on your confidence, and find ways to boost it, you'll learn to develop greater self-confidence in many areas of your life.

A Problem-Busting Tool

Confidence Booster

It's not always easy to feel confident. When you feel low and your confidence is a little shaky, grab a piece of paper and write your name at the top of it. Think about who you are as a person. Write down at least five positive personality traits that you have. Are you kind? Are you thoughtful? Are you smart or funny? Write down at least two talents that you have. Perhaps you are a gifted musician or perhaps you are good at public speaking? Maybe you're a fast sprinter? Write down three more things you like about yourself. Now you have a list of at least ten things you like about yourself. When you're feeling low and are lacking in confidence, look again at the list to remind yourself that you have a lot to feel confident about.

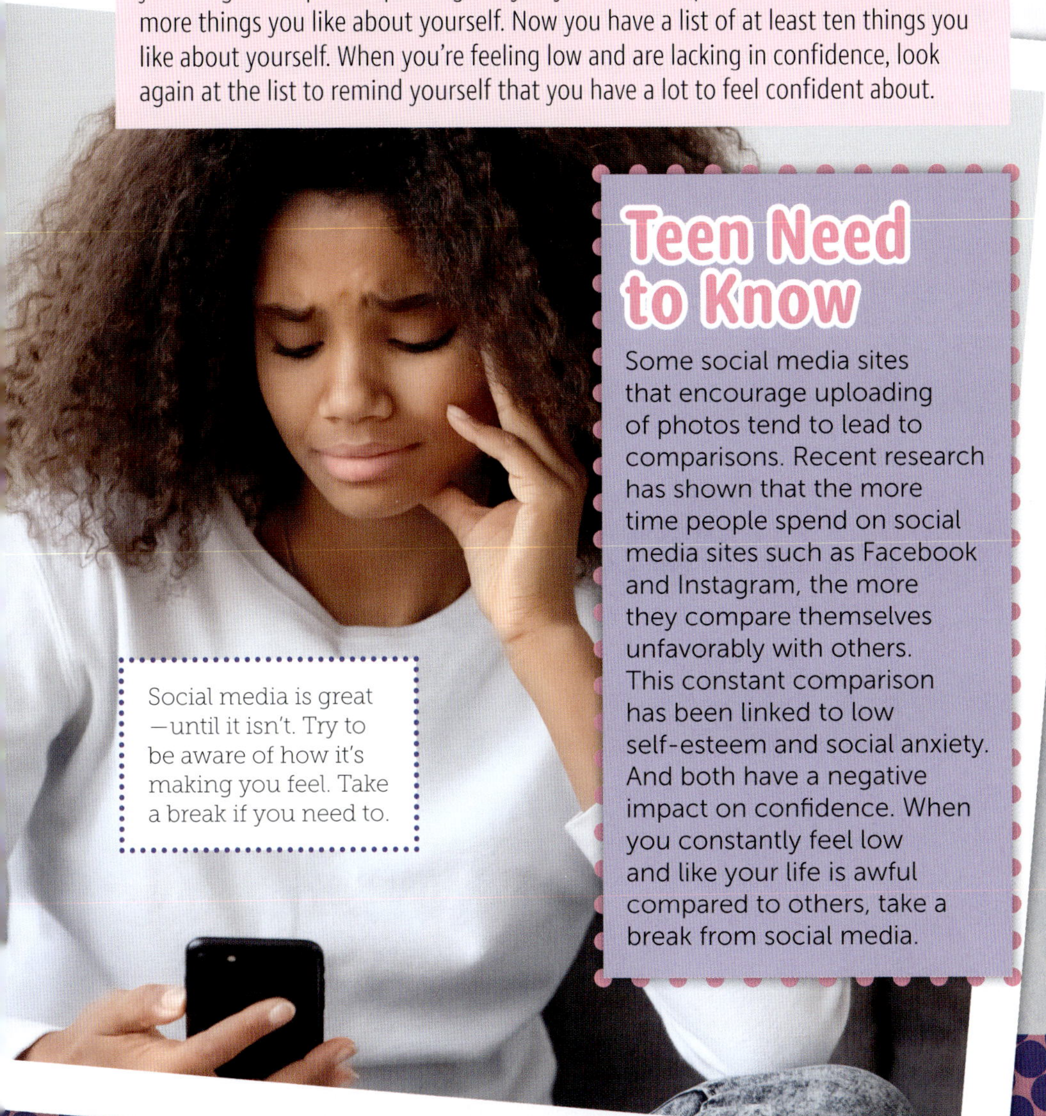

Social media is great—until it isn't. Try to be aware of how it's making you feel. Take a break if you need to.

Teen Need to Know

Some social media sites that encourage uploading of photos tend to lead to comparisons. Recent research has shown that the more time people spend on social media sites such as Facebook and Instagram, the more they compare themselves unfavorably with others. This constant comparison has been linked to low self-esteem and social anxiety. And both have a negative impact on confidence. When you constantly feel low and like your life is awful compared to others, take a break from social media.

Let's Talk about Self-Assessment

When you did the confidence-builder activity on page 33, you may have had to think hard about the things you are good at. This is because people are naturally critical. We often find it easier to see our own weaknesses, and to point out other people's weaknesses too. This is why we need to develop the skill of self-assessment.

Everyone is good at something. Sometimes, you just have to dig a little deeper to figure out what it is.

Defining Self-Awareness Skills: Self-Assessment

The skill of self-assessment challenges us to find the good and bad in ourselves. Self-assessment is having an understanding of your strengths and weaknesses so that you know both your abilities and limitations. Sometimes, you may feel bad that you have weaknesses, but everyone has them. By acknowledging them, you can work on them and continue to build on your strengths.

A PROBLEM-BUSTING TOOL

SWOT Analysis

How do you figure out what you're good at and what your strengths and weaknesses are? The first step is to take some time out and to think things through. Reflect on your past experiences and how you felt about them or what others said to you afterward. Then, you can complete a SWOT analysis like this:

- **Strengths:** What advantages do you have that other's don't (skills, education, or connections)? What do you do better than others? What do people say about your strengths? What achievements are you most proud of?
- **Weaknesses:** What do you avoid because you don't feel good at it? What do your loved ones say are your weaknesses? Do you have any bad habits? Do you have any personality traits that you see as a weakness?
- **Opportunities:** What opportunities are available to help you improve? Look at your strengths and see if these open up opportunities for you.
- **Threats:** Could any of your weaknesses lead to threats? What is standing in the way of your success? Is there anything you can do about those threats?

The Big Five

You are unique. That means your strengths and weaknesses will be different from those of your friends, siblings, and even people you have a lot in common with. But there are certain skills that can help you navigate life a little better. If you're not strong in these skills, work on them so that you become better at them:

Communication skills: Everyone needs to be able to communicate well. This includes speaking, listening, and writing.

Problem-solving skills: Identifying and working on problems is important. You can find out more about this on pages 50–53.

Decision-making skills: Making an informed and responsible decision involves gathering information. It means then thinking about the problem and the consequences of your solution.

Time-management skills: Managing your time effectively will help you prioritize the right tasks and work efficiently.

Emotional awareness: Manage your emotions. Know what causes you to feel a certain away, whether it's good or bad.

The Benefits of Self-Assessment

Knowing what your strengths and weaknesses are has many benefits. To start with, self-assessment builds confidence. When you know your strengths and accept your weaknesses, but continue to work on them, you will be more self-assured and confident. Another benefit of self-assessment is that you'll make better decisions. This is because you know what you're capable of, and what feels comfortable and right to you. It's OK to be a little out of your comfort zone, but when you know your limits, that will guide your decision-making. When you can self-assess, you'll be more resilient too. If things don't work out, you can pick yourself up and move forward with determination. And last but not least, when you understand your strengths and weaknesses, you'll be able to build better, stronger relationships because you'll know yourself better.

Overcoming Obstacles

When you know your strengths and weaknesses, you'll find it easier to embrace challenges and overcome obstacles in your path. When you're facing an obstacle, instead of shying away from the problem, think about how you can use your strengths to overcome it. Think about whether you have a weakness that is stopping you overcoming the problem. Then, develop a plan of action and put it into practice. When you're done, think about how it went. You could also ask for feedback from others to get an even better understanding. If need be, adjust the plan and try again—sometimes, you just need to figure out a better plan.

When you know what you're comfortable with, you'll know your limitations. You'll also be more willing to try new things.

No one is perfect and everyone will fail at something at some point in their lives. But how you deal with the failure is the important thing.

Lessons from Failing

For most teens, the fear of failure can be a big issue. When you're trying your best to fit in, why would you want to draw attention to your shortcomings? Why would you want to try something if you aren't sure you're going to do well at it? Let's recap what you already know: When you're pushing yourself to do something new or difficult and you don't succeed at first, that's not failing. When you don't succeed the first time round, you are learning important lessons and developing a growth mindset. And, to add to this, you're learning about yourself. You are discovering your strengths and weaknesses. These are all great things.

Teen Need to Know

Discovering your strengths and weaknesses is not a quick process, and you don't have to have everything figured out right now. You have your whole life to reflect and learn about yourself. The trick is understand yourself right now.

Making Comparisons

You've done your SWOT analysis, and have a good idea of what you're good at and what still needs some work. You may look around at school and compare yourself to others. You may think some are smarter. There may be those who are sportier. There are some students who are just really funny and sociable. Perhaps you're the life and soul of a party or perhaps you're shy and don't like to be the center of attention. It's natural for people to compare themselves to others. We look at their skills, personalities, achievements, and emotions, and then think about our own.

Research says that, typically, when you compare yourself to people and think you are better than them, you feel good about yourself and much more confident in your abilities. So what happens when you instead compare yourself to people and think they are better than you? Perhaps you look at those people's lives and think about how great they must be.

Sometimes the things you find difficult come naturally to others. That's OK. Find your own strengths.

Teen Need to Know

Sometimes, teenagers think that their strengths and weaknesses are fixed and cannot be changed. But that's not true. You are not stuck with your limitations, but you shouldn't ignore them either. If ignored, your weaknesses will become a barrier to achieving your goals. With persistence and hard work, you can work on your weaknesses and improve on them. Keep working on your strengths too, to keep them really top-notch.

You may automatically think about what they have that you don't have. You could make comparisons with their appearance and their lifestyle, and feel bad about yourself. If that happens, stop. Go back to the SWOT analysis and the confidence-builder you did earlier. Read what you wrote, pause, and try again. Remember, EVERYONE has strengths and weaknesses. And that includes you too.

In an Online Perfect World

Today's teens document their lives on social media, so it is easier than ever to make comparisons. There are photos everywhere of people's amazing lives, from vacations to food and fashion. But, social media posts can be a little *too* perfect. The problem is that for some, seeing other people's perfect lives makes them feel inadequate. They dwell on their weaknesses without seeing the value of their strengths. If you find this happening to you, pause and reflect. Take a bit of time to remind yourself of your strengths.

Did you know, 40 percent of teen social media users feel pressure to post only content that makes them look good and gets a lot of comments or likes?

Let's Talk about Accepting Feedback

One way to develop your self-assessment skills is to ask for feedback. Feedback is when someone gives you insights, observations, or evaluations about your behavior. You can ask a friend, parents, teacher, coach, or mentor for their feedback. Sometimes, you don't even have to ask, people just offer feedback anyway.

Defining Self-Awareness Skills: Accepting Feedback

The aim of feedback is to help you grow and improve. So when you accept feedback, you learn about yourself. You can apply the feedback to grow as a person. Feedback is better when it's framed constructively, but sometimes, it's not. This is when you have to dig deep and think more about *what* the person is saying than *how* they are saying it.

Listen Carefully

When someone gives you feedback, and you don't like it, take a breath before you launch into a defensive argument! Actively listen to what the person is saying and try to understand their viewpoint. Actively listening means you don't interrupt and you stay focused.

Often, other people see things differently from you, so their feedback can be really helpful.

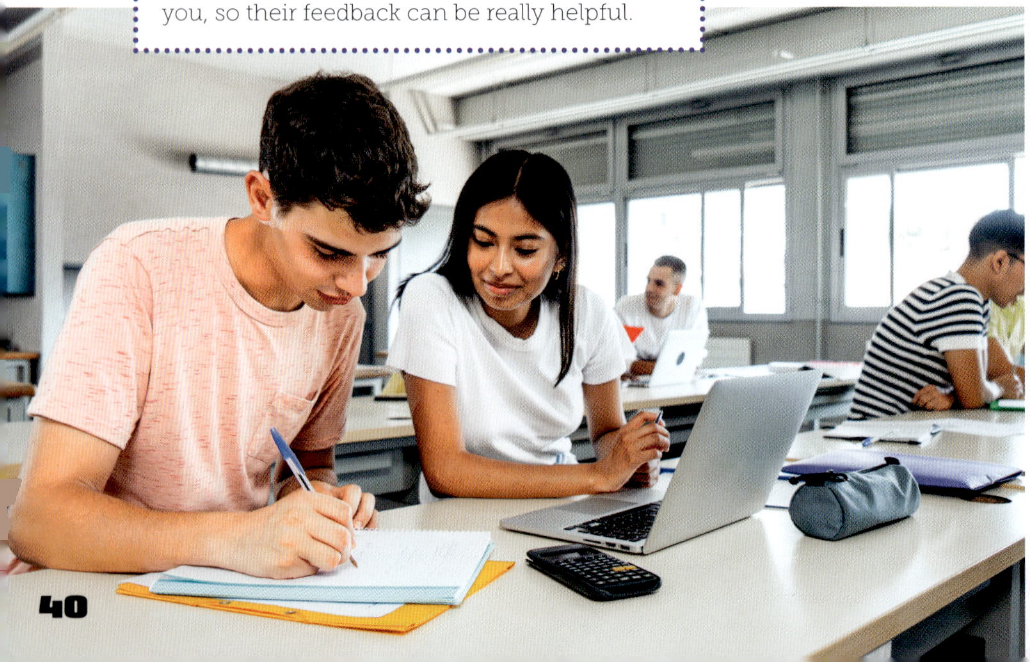

If you aren't sure what the person means, ask questions to clarify what they're saying. You don't have to agree with their feedback, but it will be helpful to reflect on what they've said. Once you've had time to think about it, try to determine if their feedback is valid. Are there clear benefits to accepting their feedback? When you've reflected, decide on the action you're going to take. It's also important to get feedback from different people. People see things differently, so the feedback from different people can be useful. Try asking a parent and friend for feedback about the same thing.

Try to see feedback as a helpful tool rather than criticism. Use it to help you grow and improve.

Building Trust and Understanding

Accepting feedback can help build trust and understanding between people. It creates openness. It develops the feeling that you can share ideas and thoughts without fear of shame. This reduces conflict and leads to personal growth. Later in the workplace, a manager is likely to give you feedback. Accepting the feedback can lead to professional growth. This is because you know what's expected of you and where you can improve in your work. All of this contributes to better mental health and improved wellbeing.

Teen Need to Know

Some teens don't want to ask for feedback. That's because they're afraid of being criticized or feeling vulnerable, but accepting feedback leads to growth. Even if someone is being negative, use your growth mindset and see their feedback as an opportunity to work on your weaknesses. If you're unsure, test the waters by asking a parent or friend for feedback first. Their feedback is more likely to be constructive and helpful.

Envisioning Your Future Self

Sooner or later you'll be starting to think about your future and what that might hold. You'll probably be thinking about college and work too, and what it will take to get there. You'll start to build plans based on that.

Let's Talk about Envisioning Your Future Self

Sometimes, your plans are short term. They're for the next hour, day, or week. For example, you may have exciting plans to exercise every day. You might plan to eat more healthily. Or you may be saving some of your allowance to buy something special. Your goals may be long term too. Although they feel far away, try to start working toward them now. For example, if you'd like to study something after school, you may need to get qualifications to do that. How will you achieve them?

Defining Self-Awareness Skills: Envisioning Your Future Self

To take the first step toward your goals, you need to envision your future self. This means thinking about what your future looks like and what you want to achieve. It means thinking about what your dreams and aspirations are. When you envision your future self, it enables easier decision making. It gives you a sense of direction, and improves your motivation.

Set Some Goals

To envision your future self, start by identifying your strengths and weaknesses. Go back to the section on self-assessment and brush up on this important skill. Now be honest with yourself and think about where you are, what is going well, and what you really want to achieve. It's time to set some goals! Think about your academic progress and set educational goals. Now think beyond school to your family life and set some goals there. What about after school and college? How do you see yourself? How are you going to get there? What do you need to do to achieve this version of yourself? Start by setting long-term goals and then add in short-term goals that will help you get where you want to be.

STUDIES IN TEEN SURVIVAL

One way to help you envision your future self is to find a mentor. A mentor is someone whom you trust to support, advise, and guide you. There are formal mentoring programs that you can join or you can simply ask an adult you admire if they'd be willing to guide you. There are many benefits to mentoring, from improved mental wellbeing to increased confidence. A study found that 74 percent of those who had mentors as teenagers said their mentor had made a significant contribution to their success later in life. Nearly 60 percent of young people acknowledged that their mentor has supported their mental health. Interestingly, 60 percent of those under 40 years old still seek advice from childhood mentors.

More than 80 percent of young people with mentors say this relationship has helped them with issues related to school and their education.

WHY SELF-AWARENESS WORKS

By being more self-aware, your day-to-day life at school, college, and work will be happier. Your mental wellbeing will improve too. This chapter has looked at four skills to help develop self-awareness: building confidence, self-assessment, accepting feedback, and envisioning your future self. Let's take a look at what we covered.

1 Confident Teens Are Willing to Try New Things

When you feel confident, you're more eager to put yourself out there. You'll also know that even if your confidence takes a knock, that's OK because there are things you can do to build it back up again.

2 Self-Assessment Is Key to Knowing Yourself

When you know your different strengths and weaknesses, you know what you're capable of and what you need to work on.

3 Teens Who Accept Feedback Are Willing to Grow

Sometimes it can be difficult to accept feedback, but feedback can help you grow and improve yourself.

4 Envisioning Yourself Helps You Set and Achieve Goals

How you see your future self, can help you set short- and long-term goals. You can work on these goals to become the person you want to be.

Turn Weaknesses into Strengths

When someone gives you negative feedback or you realize you have a certain weakness that is keeping you from being the best version of yourself, you need to take a step back. Think things through, and see how you can work on your weakness so that it becomes a strength. It may take time, but with perseverance, you will succeed.

CHAPTER 4

Friendships and the Wider World

As you get older, your friendships naturally become more important. You want to fit in and feel the sense of belonging and acceptance that comes with having friendships. When it comes to forming friendships, it is likely that you'll look for teenagers you have things in common with. They often have the same likes, dislikes, and values. Try to forge friendships with these people. Slowly but surely, you'll make good friends who will help you find your place in the world.

Finding Friends

Not everyone is outgoing and sociable. Perhaps you're shy. If you're not an "out there person," don't worry. Not everyone makes friends instantly. More often than not, building good friendships takes time. Your friendships may not always last forever either. That's a natural part of life as people change and develop. Sometimes, especially as a teenager, you may not always have the best judgment of character, and you may form an unhealthy friendship. In this set up, your friend may pressure you to do things you don't want to do or that make you feel uncomfortable. Sometimes, you don't realize or understand this until it's too late. That's why being self-aware is especially important when it comes to your friendships and your place in the world.

Form friendships with teenagers who have similar interests and values to your own.

You don't need a gang of friends. Just one or two good ones are all anyone really needs.

Creating Healthier Friendships

The more self-aware you are, the healthier your friendships will be. This is because you won't constantly seek recognition and approval from others. Rather, you will be more fulfilled and happy within yourself. You are likely to be confident too. When you focus on your own thoughts and behavior, you grow as a person. You are responsible for your own wellbeing rather than relying on others.

Upskilling to Succeed

We've looked at several self-awareness skills but there are some more skills that will be beneficial to your friendships too. These are problem-solving and impact awareness. When you understand these skills, your friendships and any other relationships will benefit.

Teen Need to Know

There are many benefits to having friends through your teenage years. Studies have shown that teens with friends have fewer symptoms of depression and have lower rates of anxiety. Having strong, healthy friendships is good for your confidence and self-esteem. You're also likely to be a more positive person, with a more optimistic outlook. All this leads to a healthier life, both mentally and physically, now as a teenager and later as an adult.

Sharing your problems with a friend is much healthier than keeping them to yourself.

Problems, Problems, and More Problems!

Have you ever noticed as you go about your day-to-day life how many different problems crop up? Just as you have one thing fixed, the next problem may arise. Sometimes, problems are small. For example, perhaps you left your homework at home. Other times, your problems are much greater, such as an illness or death in your family.

Defining Self-Awareness Skills: Problem-Solving

Solving problems means overcoming an obstacle to achieve a goal. You may not always get the outcome you'd like, but if you are equipped with problem-solving skills, you can make the best choice available to you.

Let's Talk about Problem-Solving

When you were younger, your parents probably helped solve most of your problems. But now as a teenager who is learning to be independent, you probably want to try and solve some of your problems yourself.

Finding Solutions

The first step to solving a problem is to actually realize that there is one. Ignorance is not always bliss! Try to figure out what is going on and what the underlying problem is. If it's a big problem and you start to feel overwhelmed, break it down into smaller parts so that it's more manageable. Think about what you can do to solve the problem. You can brainstorm the possible solutions. Then evaluate each solution, ruling out impossible ones. Think about the consequences of each solution. Then act on what you think is the best-possible option. Reflect on the outcome and see if you could have done things differently.

THE SELF-AWARENESS WORKSHOP

Ignoring a Problem

Not facing up to a problem can turn it into an even bigger one. Imagine this scenario, for example. Your ice hockey team is doing well, and hasn't lost a single game this season. You have just one big game to play, but it's against a really strong team that hasn't lost all season too. You and your team are training hard, but then you run into a problem with your friend, who is also on the team. You have a big argument over the positions that you play. It gets out of control, and starts to affect the rest of the team. You know that your fight with your friend could cost you the game. But you don't feel you can get past the argument, or talk about it. When your team loses on game day, you feel really bad. You realize it was probably your fault.

But what if you had chosen to confront the problem? It may not have escalated...

THE SELF-AWARENESS WORKSHOP

Same situation, but facing the issue.

Dealing with a Problem

You have just one big game to play—against a really strong team that hasn't lost all season, like your team. You and your team are training hard, but then you run into a problem with your teammate. You have a big argument over the positions that you play, and it affects the rest of the team. You know that your fight could cost you the game. After training, you tell your teammate that you are sorry. You don't want to let the team down either. You agree to get past it, and play as a strong team on the day. You work well together, and win. You feel great for your team, and good that you managed to fix the problem.

What Works Better Here?:

- You realize there is a problem and face it head-on rather than ignoring it and hoping that it will simply go away.
- You resolve the problem before it gets out of control.
- You feel good for fixing the issue, and winning the game.

Problem-Solving—What Can It Do for You?

Have you ever been in a situation like this? Did you find it hard to decide what was the right thing for you to do? When you have a problem that's getting you down, spend a bit of time reflecting on it. Carefully think through the consequences before acting on your solution.

Working as a team can help you solve problems too, because everyone sees things differently.

A PROBLEM-BUSTING TOOL

When a Problem Is Too Big

Sometimes, problems are too big for you to solve alone. That's fine and there's no shame in asking for help. Actually, knowing when you need help is a good thing. Decide who would be best to give advice. For example, this could be a friend or older sibling. It could be a trusted adult, such as a parent, teacher, or counselor. Explain your problem and if you've asked them to offer advice, listen carefully to what they say. If you still don't feel that the problem is solved, don't give up. Sleep on it and ask someone else for help.

Let's Talk about Impact Awareness

It may seem that all around you, people are facing difficult times. From wars and climate change to poverty and illness, the world may seem out of control. As a teenager, you may feel helpless. You may think that you can't really make a difference. But this isn't true. Everything you do, or don't do, has an impact, or effect, on others. That extends from your family and friends to your community, and even beyond to the wider world.

You can make a positive impact at home by helping your parents with chores.

Defining Self-Awareness Skills: Impact Awareness

Impact awareness means you consciously make an effort to understand the impact you have on others. Your impact can be positive or negative. Either way, by being aware of your impact, you will hopefully make better decisions. You are more likely to try and make a positive impact rather than affect those around you negatively.

Teen Need to Know

Psychologists sometimes talk about "emotional contagion." This phrase means when two or more people in a group feel the same thing, that emotion is passed on to others in the group. It means that emotions are contagious. Yes, they're catchy—just like a virus! Think about your group of friends. If two friends feel anxious about an exam, the chances are, their mood of anxiety becomes the mood of the group. Then, soon, everyone will start to feel anxious too.

Another example is when a person arrives at a bus stop and becomes impatient waiting for the bus. If another person shows impatience too, the rest of the group still start to act impatiently, even if they don't know each other. As you can see from these examples, emotional contagion can impact a group negatively. But in exactly the same way, it can impact a group positively too. That means you can "infect" your group of friends with a positive attitude or kindness.

Be Accountable for the Negative

Sometimes, even if you try really hard, you don't always have a positive impact on others. When you do something that has an obvious negative impact, be accountable for your actions. Being accountable means taking ownership of your actions and behavior, and if you do something wrong, you try to avoid doing it again. Sometimes, you have to do something that has a negative impact on one person but has a positive impact on others. If this is the case, take ownership and explain your actions. Although you may have upset someone, if you acknowledge this, it can help ease any tension.

If you smile at a stranger while waiting for the bus or train, that person would likely smile back.

Embrace Diversity

You can create a positive impact by embracing diversity. Diversity is the differences people have. It can include race, ethnicity, gender, age, socio-economic status, and religion. While diversity can drive people apart, when it is embraced, people's differences are celebrated. By having diverse friends, you'll learn more about other people and grow to respect their differences. Embracing diversity as a teenager means you'll be a more inclusive adult and create a positive impact in the world around you.

Each year millions of teens give up their time and talent to help others in their community or environment, creating a positive impact.

Give Back to Your Community

While you make a positive impact on your friends and family, you can extend this to your broader community. There are many ways to make a positive impact in your community.

- **Plan a community project:** Gather your friends and family and start something. It doesn't have to be big. Something small that can grow is just as worthwhile. For example, a community vegetable garden. This can help feed the community and create a sense of bonding where everyone pulls together to achieve a common cause.
- **Volunteer:** Give up your time to help others. This can be anything from working in a shelter to helping a neighbor.
- **Start a collection:** Collecting money to contribute to a cause is a good step in the right direction, and you can collect goods too. For example, set up a box at school for pet food. When the box is full, donate the contents to your local animal shelter.
- **Become a mentor:** Now that you know what a mentor is, you can be one too! Your local community center is a good place to start. It may need a teenager to help younger children with homework or to be a coach for a sports team. Start small and you'll be surprised at the impact you could make on a younger child's life.
- **Take a stand:** When you see something that upsets you and doesn't match your values, don't just watch it happen. Take a stand and speak up. You don't need to start a big protest, but you can spend time helping an organization or initiative that aligns with your values and beliefs.

STUDIES IN TEEN SURVIVAL

A global study into how teens around the world can make an impact looked at how teenagers feel about key global concerns. Of the 25,000 teens surveyed in 26 countries, 87 percent felt that they could make a difference and were motivated to do something. To the teens surveyed, poverty was the biggest concern. That was closely followed by climate change, and then sexual abuse, unemployment, and political corruption. The study also found that the more connection a teenager has to their community, the more empowered they feel to make a difference within it.

Why Self-Awareness Works

You made it to the end of the book and you've learned some great skills to help steer you on the right path to becoming more self-aware. Let's revisit solving problems and impact awareness to see what they can do for you.

1 Reflect on Your Problems

Don't just rush into solving a problem. Spend time reflecting on it and thinking about the consequences of your actions.

2 Ask for Help When You Need It

When a problem seems too big for you to solve on your own, ask for advice. If that doesn't help, keep trying until you get the best solution to your problem.

3 Being Accountable Can Minimize Negative Impact

When you realize that your actions may have had a negative impact on those around you, take ownership and be accountable. Admit your fault. This may not fix things immediately, but it can help the other people involved better understand your actions.

4

You Can Make a Difference

Every action or behavior has a consequence and creates an impact. By being empathetic and kind, as well as embracing diversity, you can create a positive impact on those around you.

Remember to Keep Learning

Working on self-awareness skills can be difficult—looking inward doesn't always come easily to teenagers. But, if you can try to get the hang of some of these skills now, you will develop into a much more self-aware adult.

CONCLUSION

Skills for Life

Now that you've started on your self-awareness journey, you need to remember that these skills won't magically happen. Try to work at them every day. Some days will also be better than others. There'll be days when you think you're a self-aware genius and other days when you feel a little clueless! That's OK. Take a deep breath and go back to chapter one. Work through each skill and brush up your knowledge. Here are some quick tips to remind you what you have learned.

Remember to Reflect and Talk

Self-reflection is important. The more in tune you are with your emotions, the easier self-awareness will be. Talking about your problems is also key. Discuss them with your friends and be open with your parents. Keep talking to the people you care about and sharing how you feel. Remember, they can help.

Being more self-aware will lead to stronger relationships and improved wellbeing.

If in Doubt, Read Again

When things feel overwhelming and you're not sure where to begin, go back to page 51 and read through the tips. Sometimes, just reminding yourself of some key strategies can help set you back on a steady path and make things seem less daunting.

Keep Going

Learning self-awareness skills will leave you feeling confident and positive in your abilities. There may be bumps along the way! But with a growth mindset and a willingness to embrace challenges, you'll learn and grow into the best version of yourself.

Share Your Skills

Remember to share what you've learned with friends and family. You've learned some powerful tools, and are in a position to help others work on their self-awareness skills. And the more everyone is on board, the healthier and happier everyone will be.

Glossary

acceptance agreeing to receive or undertake something offered

acknowledged recognized as good or important

anxious nervous or worried

aspirations hopes or ambitions of achieving something

benefits the advantages a person gains from something

biases preferences not based on fact or experiences

clarify to make a statement less confusing

comfort zone a situation or position where a person feels secure, comfortable, and in control

communication sharing information with others

comparisons finding similarities and differences between things

confidence a person's sense of security in their abilities, qualities, or ideas

conflict a disagreement or argument

consciously deliberately and intentionally

constructively in a way that is useful or beneficial

critical describes someone who expresses disapproving comments or judgments

criticism judgments of the good and bad in something

defensive anxious to avoid criticism

depression a mental illness in which a person has a low mood and lack of interest in most activities

determination having a strong desire to do or achieve something

empathetic being able to understand and share the feelings of another person

flexible able to change

halfsiblings the children of a person's biological parent and a stepparent

hormones chemicals in the body that help the organs function properly

ignorance lack of knowledge or information

impulsive carrying out action without thinking carefully about it beforehand

inadequate insufficient

independent not requiring help

limitations something that restricts a person

motivation the process that enables a person to achieve their goals

obstacle something that blocks a person's way or progress

optimistic hopeful and confident

overwhelmed feeling overpowered by emotions and thoughts

ownership taking responsibility for something

persistence continuing in spite of difficulty or opposition

personality traits the thoughts, feelings, and actions that make people different from one another

phobia a fear of something

productive able to do something effectively

psychologists professionals who study the human mind and the behaviors and thoughts of people

purpose determination

recognition acknowledgement

reflect to think carefully about something that has happened

reluctant unwilling or hesitant to do something

self-assured when a person is confident in their abilities or character

self-conscious when a person feels overly aware of themself

self-esteem confidence in your own worth or abilities

self-talk the way you talk to yourself

siblings brothers and sisters

socio-economic status the social standing of a person based on their education, wealth, and occupation

stepparent the person a divorced parent marries

stepsiblings the children of a stepparent

support network the people in a person's life that help them achieve their goals

time-management skills skills that help a person manage their time effectively

valid reasonable and believed to be true

values morals and beliefs

volunteer to offer to do something without being forced to do it

Find Out More

BOOKS

Daniels, Grace. *Life Skills for Teenage Boys: How To Manage Money, Be Confident, Make Friends, Communicate, Develop Relationships, Set Goals, Cook, Clean and Become an Independent Young Adult.* Okanagan Lifelong Learning Press, 2023.

Higgins, Jenn. *Teen Girl's Survival Guide.* Canyon Press, 2022.

Schab, Lisa M. *The Self-Esteem Workbook for Teens: Activities to Help You Build Confidence and Achieve Your Goals.* Instant Help, 2022.

WEBSITES

Learn more about the importance of self-awareness at:
https://betterkids.education/blog/what-is-self-awareness-and-why-is-it-important

For information and resources on teenage health and wellbeing, visit Stars Youth at:
https://starsyouth.net/mind-body-soul

ORGANIZATIONS

For more help with self-awareness, explore this organization:

Teen Lifeline, PO Box 10745, Phoenix, AZ 85064
602 248 8337
Website: teenlifeline.org

Publisher's note to educators and parents:
All the websites featured above have been carefully reviewed to ensure that they are suitable for students. However, many websites change often, and we cannot guarantee that a site's future contents will continue to meet our high standards of educational value. Please be advised that students should be closely monitored whenever they access the Internet.

Index

About the Author

Jennifer Sanderson has written books on many different topics, from tennis and baby animals to geography and self-care. She has two teenagers who, like all young people, are learning to navigate life's ups and downs by becoming more in tune with themselves. She's hoping this book will give them and other readers the skills they need to go from the roller coaster of being teenagers to fully-fledged self-aware adults.